Same Blue Chevy

BY
GALE
RENÉE
WALDEN

TIA CHUCHA PRESS
CHICAGO

ACKNOWLEDGMENTS

Some of the original versions of these poems appeared in the following magazines:
The Laurel Review, Harvard Review, The New Review, Puerto Del Sol, Soundings East, Spoon River Quarterly & Sun Dog.

"Dreaming of Dogs" takes its title from a musical composition of Mr. Robert Scott Wigton.

Thanks to the Art Institute of Chicago for a sustaining presence. Paintings accessed from their collection for this collection include: Edward Hopper's "Nighthawks," Rene Magritte's "Time Transfixed," Paul Delvaux's "Village of Sirens," and the work of Ivan Albright.

Thanks also to Mary Clark, Peggy Flyntz, Jody Stewart, and David Wallace. Extreme gratitude is extended to the Ragdale Foundation for time & space to write and to Patty Jo & Don for just about everything.

ISBN 1-882688-10-4
Library of Congress Catalog Card Number: 96-60118

Book design: Jane Brunette
Cover painting: "On the Road to Pearl's Dinner" by Paula Wittner
Back cover photo: Rod Kessler

PUBLISHED BY:
TIA CHUCHA PRESS
A Project of the Guild Complex
PO Box 476969
Chicago, IL 60647

DISTRIBUTED BY:
NORTHWESTERN UNIVERSITY PRESS
Chicago Distribution Center
11030 S. Langley
Chicago, IL 60628

Funding for this project was partially provided by the National Endowment for the Arts, the Illinois Arts Council, and the Lannan Foundation.

To My Sisters,
Joelle & Michelle

Table of Contents

Part ONE

Part
two

Part
three

Part
one

"But this was Saturday, it was lazy
the Beatles were singing
how much they loved me."

Moving

A preacher's family doesn't own anything
except its mobility and the picture
of a white-haloed Jesus.
Tomorrow night, someone else's daughter
will walk to the empty church
and hit the light to the stained glass
so that everyone within a mile
can see the angel pointing to the sky.

In the neighborhood, fat women play percussion
plopping sausage and dumplings into oil
while others sweep pavement to sand.
My mother, red-haired and modern, says,
Good riddance to this Old World. Everyone
speaks of America in hushed tones
as if it were a God whose throne
they had inherited.

No longer a child, I
still miss the angel and move
every other month, wondering about mountains,
what other people do at night.
I try to imagine myself old
but it's beyond me, and each time I leave

I prepare myself for a colorful past, waiting
for an extraordinary shadow
to settle into light.

Rebirth

Just this:
　　　　that someone bled you once
　　　　simply to see blood,
that once you walked into
　　　　a room, all woman.
There was a man waiting
　　　　who took you
　　　　took you
for yourself and you took
back the green waking
　　　　of your mother
　　　　exiting the South
　　　　via a rocky cave.
You could see her
moving past history
　　　　into herself
as the camera followed
　　　　a narrowing staircase
toward the night.
　　　　It started her
in the direction
　　　　freedom might have led anyway
　　　　and it didn't matter
　　　　that along the way

someone called her "whore"
as she parlayed suitcases
            brown leather, canvas, stripes,
into all those decisions of
shoes and perfumes.
            What daughter
wouldn't have loved her then
            the brown clunky pumps
echoing down an empty railroad
            as she made her way North
direct, toward the idea of you.
            She would have wished
more for you
            than this room—
            a story to tell
your own daughter
            that begins with the opening
of a door and traverses
a circular, glistening staircase.
It never goes down
            you will tell her
and there will be nights
            when you can ascend
so far the stars will frighten you:
            I cannot lie to you,
to your side
all day long there will be rooms
filled with acts you will want to deny
the journey out, steep,
stairs counting down
like the Bible:
Genesis, Exodus, Leviticus.

The first step is the hardest
            but remember
it is never the beginning:
the mother's opening line,
"and you were born,"
never ending.

Marquette Park, 1966

When the call came
my mother was washing her dyed hair
in beer, as a conditioner & topic for gossip,
          alms for a congregation
who expected a preachers wife
          to be thin with prayer & smell of
orchids & gardenias.
But this was Saturday, it was lazy
          the Beatles were singing
how much they loved me.
          Outside in the streets the
neighborhood Polish
shouted frantic & loose
as children played hopscotch
          jumping down the block
to Sky Blue
where city trinkets were on display
and the butcher wrapped kilbaska
in white paper for barbecues.

The message on the phone was simple:
                    they are coming to your church with the King
                    they will want to go in and pray

and suddenly my father was back
rushing around like the emergency of something about to happen
bolting next door to the church to unlock the double wooden doors
leading to Sanctuary.
My father was thirty-two & handsome
        and the clerical collar he wore
propped him up higher than the rest of us
        so that when he lifted me
I went all the way to the ceiling
        which was pretty close to God.
He didn't lift me that day; I was eight
        and getting harder to hold.
Three girls trailed him to the door
        trying to catch his legs
as he forgot to wave good-by.

When the first rock went through
the parsonage window
my mother reached for the phone
called June, the only neighbor she trusted
and my mother who never left the house without makeup or high-heels
who told me I'd be thirty before I'd understand the true beauty of lipstick
wrapped a towel around her head, barefoot opened the door
unto a crowd of people:
        Butcher, Baker, Locksmith, Thief.
The woman two doors down
who wore pink cashmere
whose daughter was named
after a Christmas Carol was there.
She was the mother we all coveted
and I started to smile at her

but she had changed
into something way past herself
                Nigger Lovers
she screamed.
My mother looked straight through her & expanded,
grew large enough to shelter us all below her skirts;
              zig-zagged us
into the clear open Oz
            of the city street
as we jumped the rough blacktop
into the thin hands of June.

June walked us up the third floor flat
and led us to the screened-in porch
where her daughter Karen waited.
The first shot was distant as a cork-pop.
We looked to Karen for guidance;
she was Catholic and we needed ritual
so we turned three times & faced East
and then we could see the shadowed,
distant surge of the crowd as they started
to rock Impalas as if they were toy models
in a Japanese horror film.

The shouting & cursing merged with the singing marchers
and the voices & songs echoed into us, becoming our own.
The marchers never got to the church
that day—the roads were blocked and
the city had started to burn again.
           On Sunday the pews were empty in church and
           my father preached the sermon
about loving your neighbor to his family alone

while my mother sang the hymns in
a thin, melodic line.
Outside the Christian Soldiers
                    marched onward
                    and the streets
rang out a music
                    of guns
that never ended.

The children chose alternative codas:
                    some turning
themselves in early
                    taking their colors
to the graves.
Others didn't grow up
                    because they had seen the outcome
but none of us ever really went home again
to the city of our dreams
where the double-dutching
of black & white
                    was too pretty to leave
                    and the earnest prayers of children
assured that it was not only the cinematic monster
looming visible over skyscrapers
& small quilted farmlands
that was guaranteed, by the end, to fall.

Everyone's Living Room

This is what happens at night in Normal:
children marry wrong, everyone quits smoking,
and fathers love their daughters so fiercely
everywhere it is quiet. In houses wrapped
with porches, rocking chairs are wearing treads
in wood as people remember the first time,
which has become your first time,
which has become your fear. Inside
telephones are ringing and people watch
the ten-o'clock news—there it is safe
to love sentimentally, there it is common
to fight without valor, and when a globe
hits the bedroom wall you can be sure
someone is naming a hurricane
and you are not immune.
Tonight, in some city, a criminal
will strike, but in Illinois
you are in everyone's living room
so why, passing through, does it surprise you so
to look past curtains, through lit glass
and see a young woman—
face blank as an angel's
bent before one man—
an altar,
pretending to be us all.

Each New Moon

It's someone.
Going somewhere—
Illinois perhaps
or Michigan.
He is hitchhiking
or shouting. He is
turning away from you
slow as a millstone
which does not explain
the sincere darkness
of the inside
of cars
or how an innocent
switch of the radio
causes a love
you had forsaken
to emerge
from the night
hitting the car
with the force of an animal.

Traveling moves like this:
each new moon
follows the road

like a dog
and every town
crumples behind you.
You are moving
which does not explain
why in certain ways
everything has stopped.
He is gone
and now it's Kansas.
There are brick streets
and houses and
you have no home
but there are people
on porches they have
been on forever
waving you in
calling, it could
be yours, it could
all be yours.

From the Porch

Everything is blond: the sky,
the wheat, the branch of hair
sweeping your eyes as you bend
to examine the fence
that has been falling
for such a long time.
It must be a love of ongoing decay
that keeps your fingers
caressing the wood, collecting splinters,
and when you shake the pickets
as if to force a decision,
I try to memorize each angle
of your body, the direction
each shaft of wheat
is turning. This
is where I have come to—
outside with the laundry,
the dogs, your faith,
and because I have seen this moment
so many times, because
I have never before
believed it existed,
I look hard.
Already the moments burn,

smoking through screen doors,
drifting for years
before settling on mantles
and rockers,
invisible grandfathers,
convinced, immovable,
waiting to be proven wrong.

The Falling of Objects

How little I remember. Maundy Thursday
each minute growing darker. Before
at a table, Christians and Jews
in that slip of history, where, masquerading
as sadness, the future predicted itself,
rearranged seats, and we began transformation
into those who would be able to live it.
It's not always that big. Forget
recognition; the voice is where
the heart sits, and I confess
I too have darkened rooms, pulled shades
merely to be able to open
and hear from some other place
"let there be light."

Childhood. And then too—
the voice. "Don't strut.
It does not become you."
Up and down like rhythms
of the crazed. "Don't strut.
Didn't a fish tell you
you should be walking in
the ways of Wise Men? Carefully,
searching only for an appropriate star."

A train again. A green shirt
and you slouching away like a Jesuit.
The train leaves. I take company.
Listen. One says, *you love the past*,
another, *other days, floral curtains*
and beside me on a tapestry seat,
large and gay, "Honey, I never fly.
Up there the world forgets itself.
Trees look like grass." The Doppler
wavers in the night and at every station
I believe I see you on the tracks.
What has your life been like?

Chicago and the devil is walking Van Buren;
would not stop for Elvis himself, cheeks
puffed out, the hands like wings keeping
the pace of symphonies. Wooden horses
up and down. Round and round. And
what is the world but rhythm?
So we beat on. On the embankment, hobos.
Wastes of fire and the smell of deceit.
And I too loved them all.
Put the same face on each.
And we were silent and worshipped.
Were overcome by someone saying
something isn't right. And he went.
He went further. And from the past, "Don't
strut. You should be praising the Lord
and not forgetting the necessary elements
of the world."

It's a thin narrative. Life and still no place

for the falling of objects. Short white octopi.
The china doll. Then ancient singing.
The distance of the moon gate swinging. The dogs.
The sinking. The churches growing darker, darker;
that perfect ceremony of leaving. And
what is there left?
Anthems are being sung.

My Mother's Voice

Mornings my mother would call in
voice fresh as rivers
some sort of message for my day.
It started out innocent—
"The early bird gets the worm,"
then grew ominous—
"Measure once, cut twice."

I awoke from the deep sleep
of a fourteen year old girl
into the dreams of some future else
hanging off a verge of cliffs
to hear her voice calling in:
"who will buy the cow if you can get the milk for free?"
It only caused me to burrow in deeper.

Later I thought I had learned the code
and would shout, "Waste not, want not,"
but the rules had changed
and now the voice produced direct warning
against early descent
into that land where we all call back,
the canyon where we are bound
to echo, eternally,
whatever we cannot translate.

Parents Developing

She is beautiful
and he loves her.
They are going to Europe
and he is wearing the same
baggy pants which have
become your uniform
and still she appears
in your dreams
wearing pink and carrying
a series of symbols
you don't quite get—
lambs and houses, cashmere,
perfume and pearls,
strands that threaten
to float off, entwine
your neck and
maybe for once
it's right
you are back here
in rooms you
weren't allowed to inhabit.

In the picture
his smile makes

your heart bump
with a speed
that says, you
could easily have been
her. Could have
understood devotion
but instead
they have birthed you
have given a certain
weight to the
mystery that
surrounds your life
and surely
they must have carefully
picked the details
that would compose their own:
the God they follow,
the blood soup ladled when poor,
some child in an attic
who will be forever
trespassing against them.

Part two

"The houses on our block were white.
On the television, the war, constant,
but outside on the street, a selfish joy.
None of these boys was going to go."

Cecil and Jonson

Cecil is in love with a ball. Disturbingly and emphatically in love with a ball. When the ball is in the air, everything is ball. All is ball. The universe exists tiny, round, hurdling. The ball is an object, therefore innocent. It is, in fact, more precisely, the game of ball that Cecil is in love with. Ball on earth is obsession; ball in air is a way of life. When the ball is in the air, Cecil can jump like a Russian gymnast. Cecil can be perfect when the ball is in the air. I have only been obsessed with the absence of things in the way that Cecil is obsessed with the ball. I have searched the sky for hours to give location to loss, and somewhere I have been perfect.

Jonson has been in love with Cecil for a long time now, but because Jonson is dog, not ball, her charms have eluded Cecil. Jonson does not understand the game. This is how things go for her: Ball is thrown, Cecil runs after Ball, Jonson runs after Cecil. Ball exists for Cecil. Cecil exists for Jonson. Sometimes, by accident, Jonson catches the ball in her mouth and Cecil runs after Jonson, but really it is after Ball. Now Jonson has become part of the game. At night I bring Jonson in and Cecil cries at the door. Jonson, on the other side, worries about Cecil. I worry about Jonson. I worry that she doesn't understand.

Dreaming of Dogs

The houses are quiet.
Men come with animals
and squat in the bushes.

Inside, you sit in the chair,
arms unfolding the secrets,
your legs stretched out, wanting more

saying, I'm not guilty:
I didn't know the rules.
It was a mistake meant only for you.

Shadows of trees
hang from the sky, scrape
against windows. Far away

cats howl to each other,
their one mating call.

We've all known this would happen.
One day the outside doesn't open up.
Rooms divide into smaller rooms.

In the chair, you are too human.

Somewhere off in the darkness
gold dogs are running wild through woods.
Their eyes are yellow
and buildings don't matter.
They don't stop; don't speak.

A knock at the door. You stand up straight.
I roll on the floor, begging.
Outside scratching.

My ears hear too much. Your hands
stretch toward the door. My tongue
reaches out. Touches wood.

Scars

City kids get them—
the knife across the face or ear
one slash—you're a man
some smart-aleck crack
somebody's bad day
and no one can sleep
because at night
there are dark things
crashing near the airport.

He makes up stories, they amuse him.
He talks of the war
as if he had been there.
Women like these wounds he tells her.
Men who don't have the real things
get tattoos.

He talks of passing through
panes of glass.
He becomes one of the birds
that fly against their window
thinking perhaps all clarity
is the same, not realizing,
till the last second the thump,
the drop, the feel of solid ground.

Misguided Angels

That summer the women sat on their porches
waving fans at cars passing.
A yellow Dodge Dart, the ugly pink Olds.
The boys in the street were playing
several things having to do with balls,
balls bouncing, rebounding, rolling
in the air, or on ground. Heat.
This was 1972 in the city.
The houses on our block were white.
On the television, the war, constant,
but outside on the street, a selfish joy.
None of these boys was going to go.

In the midst of old women on stoops
and children gliding through hydrant rivers,
what I hoped for was undefined.
That was the year each boy I touched
had smoothly veiled skin. Driving
from the city to prairies outside town,
we would sit on car hoods, a bottle of Blue Nun
between us, until the boy, silly with rock & roll
and small insincere punches, would
suddenly become reverent, look to the sky
and point out Orion,

unhinged sword hanging,
nipples posing as a shield.
It was foreplay for a kiss.
I thought it a tactic
learned at a secret school for boys,
an efficient segue between hormones & romance,
romance & hormones, the cosmos thrown in,
but I too would look to the stars, acquiesce.

■

Long after street lights came on
the men who thought America infallible,
like a President or a father,
stayed on porches smoking
and yelling for their long-haired sons
to come back home, lifting immigrant arms
to the warrior of night.

One man on our block I barely knew
came all the way back to my door
saying he was in a minefield and my face
had risen like a balloon.
He said this meant he loved me
and maybe I'd consent to be his bride.
I was fifteen and I didn't like the idea
of any part of me over there,
but he was shaking
and I had been taught to be kind;
I spoke of school and my boyfriend
who was Italian and jealous.
The man went away and for months

I'd see him from my window
limping up and down the block
until he started drugs and the limp
syncopated with a shuffle,
a kind of derelict two-step.

One night it was summer again
and we woke to trash cans banging
like Timpanis, bouncing
off potholes and rolling down the street.
One by one little lights went on
like a village, and suddenly
everybody was all together again
watching him. He was luminous,
whatever drug he took was burning off
reflected in the dark, orange sky
and we cheered him silently,
cheered the visible damage done,
but when the men in uniforms
took him away,
he didn't say Vietnam
he said my name.

■

I awoke from a certain decade
tracing names in a black mirror.
The civil lines of the world warped
as the village expanded
to tangle names and faces—
betrayal no longer purely political
as the future unclaimed

walked a deserted street.
I married everyone,
as if that would help,
bride & grooms
we bravely marched down the aisle
to ungloried defeat.

Tonight in the desert
Orion hovers above
a constellation of memory
transformed into history
(lofty myth) changing
judgments & directions
until I am looking back, up, beyond
the Midwest, toward
a prairie of unscarred boys
who somehow already knew
what warriors we were destined
to become on our way to love.

The Addict's Lament

At the beach in Revere, he appears
thin, balding and shaky,
holding a baby he says, right off,
is the only reason he is alive today.

So much for chit-chat.
I'm drawn in again
past ancient shorelines
& trainless iron gazebos
to the swirling vortex that calls
on the center of his life.

"It got bad," he confesses.
"At least it's over," I say,
and we both feel bad
I have lied in front of the ocean.
"At least I keep moving," he says,
smiling, pointing to a rusty van in the lot.

And again he turns away from me
everything switching places
as his back recedes and
we each continue the journey toward
continual refrain:

I am always thinking about you.
I am always thinking about you.

After the Village

Each Victorian woman sits in a row of silence.
The dresses are shades of grey & green.
On the coast, unending blue houses,
rooftops like cornfields, the ice-caps white,
 an ocean missing rage.
The lives of mermaids & farmers
resist interpreting, so just wait.
Cackles. Corn. Hats of Easter.

Once each had been the type of woman
who loved the form of her family
shaped on a clothesline blowing.
Now, like everyone waiting to be touched
they are on the edge, faithless & full of ritual.

Behind each and every one, a shadow
of the missing, lengthening;
now families cross the country
in Nash Ramblers calling names
into prairies: Early Meadow Rue,
Mandrake, Star of Bethlehem.

At the seaside, other women are transformed.
Because he was, is, says, *in love with her,*

her body lacks gravity, weight, &
he moves to another picture entirely—
a wearied seaman quoting,
"Heavy the Oar of He who is tired,
Heavy the Coat, Heavy the Sea."

My shapes change also.
At once I am an acrobat,
and then, see, confident.
So simple, the language
of image:
Long Blond Hair.
The United States.
Or the tale of the criminal
released, pure, lacking past
reinventing for the world another man.

Or she released, painted by dawn.
Or she unknown, shadowed by noon.
Or the myth of a woman
leaving a man
becoming a fish
becoming the sea,
flesh into liquid
a moon pulling
one voice calling;
Cast out your net.
Forget your life.
Come in.

Open Lands

In the reverent prairie
the little red fox sleeps
away from the skulk.
Beyond the prairie
the city has not yet burned
or it is burning

or it is ash beginning to rise.
The sundial trails
linguistic gardens:
wood, willow, wash.
The statues are all
a perfect shade of Dresden Blue.

This is the way an innocent man
falls in love: through
centuries and skeletons of trees
stopping at the edge
where a bluebird nests
and it is safe to raise a family.

Trains recede toward
a block of houses
boxed up with light

like a child's painting
of the curious separate
form of America.

Still, safe in the repose
of a girl upstairs reading
the windowed attic beckons beyond
into a night of winded prairies
sweet everlasting
wild phantom brides.

Prophecy

They walked on the moon
when I was eleven
and even before the days
of continual replay
the bubbled man bounced again
& again onto foreign land
constrained by NASA's cord.

The bounce was no more mystical
than the skip on the school walk home
littered with lilac or red maple,
a leisurely stroll toward the year
my body grew into a gown of silver
and I reached beneath the pink night fog
to claim the floating ash.

After that I was way past thinking about cheese.
Sometimes when I thought love would return
someone would ask did I believe in the man
in the moon too and for the sake of image
I conceded that the small step
for mankind was filmed in Nevada.

Now small lights of the city
guide airplanes shooting down
and I see your face luminous
in the darkened streets of lampposts
as the moon beautiful & horrific
hangs from the sky
like the circle you drew in sand
which says you cannot be left.

Again

Light falls through the window with its familiar
repetition of afternoon. There are tomatoes,
a glass of water, an arrangement of dried weeds.
I understand your still life at the table,
your face arranged easily among objects. Everyone
must be careful not to disturb this picture.

Careful not to disperse light
through a prism and send it bouncing throughout
the house, repeating patterns, which
manifest on walls in slats of white so thin
our lives could filter through them.

If I could choose, I would choreograph tonight—
each step a pirouette crossing the ballroom floor
as we avoid repeating the mistake under a strobe
that flashes darkness & light.
But dancing is never simple.

I once saw a dance where each movement
was repeated. A ballet expanded in a regress
of mirrors—arms and legs reproduced themselves
and the dance grew into more than desire
until scarves dropped and movement ceased.

Our life is an arrangement of movements so complex
even Bach would be proud, so I can't say why the
light hitting your face reminds me of loss,
or why any of this reminds me of dance, or
why I suddenly feel a need to move to the table,
bow my head and say grace.

Part **three**

*"Memory is just desire
reversed. Same blue Chevy."*

At the Movies

Everything that we have done
has been done before. The stained satin
curtains ascend and who really knows which came first—
the hand or the image of the hand reaching over.
But there it is only the girl who lost
heart. And her (we'll call her Ida)
in the mirror, watching the fabric of her body.
Here the future is finite
and there, look, a checkered past returns.
Marble tops, silken scarf and thee.
Wood on wood. Patches on quilts.

Watch, the frame moves into a darkness of forest.
The restless eyes of animals—
dark little hitlers. The hand.
Its knife. She won't do it
She will. It drives me crazy.
This narrative created or un.
This which has risen as history
as proof of the fallibility of math—
A will equal B but who knows
what will happen to the audience of C.
Here. I have taken one thousand lovers
each one more alike than the last

on and on in some theory of diminishment.
And then the self turning in on itself,
so trite it's true. Memory is just desire
reversed. Same blue Chevy.

In the painted room a child cries.
Ida, her golden hair, her ashen hair,
awaits the men who will surely arrive.
Black boots and buckles.
She won't do it, of course.
The knife is a slim weapon against history.
The edges remain unwritten, the ballpoint,
the camera, stopped. The gas of ghosts
and the children who won't be born.
And then that jolt. My darling
you see, it is so simple.
The blue mask fits.
The scenery can be revised or denied
but here are those (the rose falling off)
who feel only from a distance,
for what is sanity but a measure of distances?

There the windows are washed in fear and
outside the forest mist rises;
it must be this reprieve of landscape
which allows for brief reverie—gauzy young women
play croquet at dawn, while elsewhere
silhouettes march into chambers
and somewhere in history your hand
my dear, remains touching. Is it real?
Lift the shade. The curtain.
Break the mirror or don't.

O image!
What dark country
     full

         ravished

                  moon.

Beauty in an Incomplete Form

I.

Here is a picture of her, twirling;
she is standing over a sewer and
a rigged fan is blowing the air up.
The air blows up, the legs move apart,
and her white pleated skirt begins waving
into loins. And now the photograph
is changing. And now she is slowly
disappearing, fading into the place
where the unknown becomes more unknown.
Years later only the loins
are still there, floating up.
The air is still, the voice we create . . .

II.

In Convent School they taught about rivers—
the flow, tight cycles of life, passage, death,
passage, life; Kings hunting children until
there was Jesus at the river calling
everyone to come and bathe.
People forgot their children in the reeds and tiny bodies
slept while the world faded from one scene
to the next. It wasn't just me
who woke to the sound of convertibles,

pink rooms filled with blond wigs,
a breeze blowing soft as sleep.

III.
For beauty I suffered subtle crosses and betrayals.
Love gone bad and my eyes prettied
with remorse. There are those who say
I dreamed myself, created and destroyed,
but I say who wouldn't have chosen
to wake spinning in the one direction
that would unravel wise men—
Kings and baseball players,
men who shouldn't have been
able to come undone.

IV.
This is what it's like to be beautiful:
white roses twirling into
the pond of a man's mind.
Here, I am not there. Here,
the light is such that I could almost
fly into other worlds: the cells
where nuns bend, keep the vows,
forget how to love. And the lies
of men bearing silences and candles
and the chanting, only Jesus.
My voice repeating, only Jesus
would have been enough for me.

Twister

A globe light shines onto the porch
as a woman in white descends
from the kitchen and kisses your head
with a grace you didn't imagine existed
until just now and you know
this is America, full of light and women.

But the midwest grew larger and misplaced itself;
cornfields bowed
to women in heels
who clicked and flickered like emeralds
and it was good
until the tornado came.

It twisted the meaning of things,
scattered young men everywhere.
Some went to college or New York City
others just tumbled off to war—
somewhere labeled somewhere else.

We come of age, preparing to leave
our promises, but when, in Managua,
watching barefoot women lighting candles
we're drawn back

to rooms filled with blue carpets,
shaded lamplight,
we know there's no escape:
Dorothy clicks her red shoes.

The Archaeologist of Frank

It starts out simple, this understanding
this male to female ratio
negotiated over the salad bar
foreshadowed by beets, and later
his hands, thin, on the piano, playing Brahms.

Every boy inside a man knows that in the bottom
of the sea of cereal lies a treasure—
a decoder ring that can signal one love
across valleys, prairies, cities—
blinking on and off into the history
of her who waits for him.

This is what Mary understands in aisle 7
in the Star Market in Watertown
watching Frank in front of the cereals:
a toy is involved. And from the moment
of definitive choice, past frozen foods and bag boys,
desire is a room where dreams are checked.

In the kitchen Frank is the archaeologist
of Captain Crunch, diving deep
into wreckage for a top striped like a tiger
perpetually spinning around a boyhood tree.

On linoleum the top disappoints.

Mary is the archaeologist of Frank,
looking past thawing meat on the counter
past the blueberries staining the table
deep into the historical playgrounds and sidewalks
that lead up to, and away from, her.

What else could cause a woman to rise
from her bed under blue moon to scatter
Lucky Charms throughout the house: green clover
yellow stars, and (complete) announce to a sleeping man:
the prize works. It is hidden. It is here.

Pauline

What a bad trick to age into a world
where the white woman isn't chic anymore,
where cancer has wormed its way into cocktail parties.
If you could have seen me then—
I tell you this is true:
I was pretty.
I wore a silk scarf. I knew
about men, which drinks they liked,
how their wives had remained little girls.
And I could dance! And then,
the pauses at the sequined blouse,
all those fumblings near dawn.
I was so sophisticated.
To look at me
you would have thought
I had never been a child.

Nighthawks

It's only the glass bending
inward and the solid alone of
"Man in Fedora, Drinking Coffee"
which makes you return again and again.
A light exactly blinding.
Outside, reflected, the shadow etches into itself
changes dimensions, makes you talk meaning.
But inside, behind the counter,
the hash cook is redefining art—
not the form of the self curving
more the slant of the ordinary—
salt, pepper, the catsup bottle unturned.

Even as it diminishes (no one else is so lucky)
the shadow looms in imagination and —abracadabra—
manifests: a couple at a counter with Solitude,
the cliché unendingly beginning.
A telescope.
Happy. Happy. Happy.
Daylight approaching the river.
A single chord rising. Then pianos.
The jag of her smile.
"Say maybe he loved her." "Well maybe he did."

Haven't you been taught all along
that the clock, when thrown from a train
is silenced? The train disappears blinking
only to reemerge on the museum wall
where the absence of clocks is always significant.

Deceptive isn't it? This which poses as past,
which poses as art, a slight hiccup in time
into a world where Bogart
is taking a non-cancerous drag.
"How could we not have known?"
the voice ticks again and again,
an off-beat more gently,
"how could we have known?"

On the magnificence of deserted city streets:
a saxophone, one patent leather shoe
tapping on aluminum buildings.

Explanation of An Affair

Her eyes were black, he said.
They reminded him of a line he had heard
about marriage and dancing
coyotes just beyond the dim light of the porch.

They reminded him of a line he had heard
about Mozart in the mesquite
coyotes in the dimmed light of the porch
lipstick on wine glasses.

It was D minor he had heard the mesquite play.
It was specific air; creosote and juniper.
Those stains on the glasses broke his heart.
What was he to do, and where?

The creosote the juniper the air
it all seemed contrived.
What was he to do? Her hair shadowed
her left eye then suddenly she turned.

All right there was still a way out.
The shadow of her had not touched him yet.
He thought of graveyards, those sacred warehouses.
He remembered the dual covering of earth over the married

and in the graveyard he didn't see her stone:
but her eyes were black, the hungry ghosts
were loose, coyotes were dancing on white tombs
and marriage was just beyond the dim light of the porch.

Waking

Listen baby, the moon
doesn't always rise.
I have heard things
about you.
And to think
I did believe you
like a tomb—
worshipping an
emptiness removed
and then set back.
Salvation
you are sleeping
refusing to take
that breath, which
like a knife
would wake you.
Now it's dark
and you are rising
over a city
waving with candles
while on the street below
the drummer boy
still parades
repeating his

one pretty speech:
Draw in. Draw in like
fevers of children.
The wolves have arrived.
I am alive.
I am no
fool.

Positions of Prayer

I.

I kneel at the foot of my bed
and always God is above,
grand and distant, like a movie
where it is Christmas in New York
and on Thirty-Second street, She
(the sales clerk) falls in love
with He (the good father, son,
a consumer to beat all consumers)
and here God is an unknown camera man,
a miracle of angles and desire.
Or the film reverses
a sparrow descends
splattering yellow
and it's left to the children:
bury the bird, contrive a rain dance.
All those songs, hands clasped tight,
the pounding of tiny feet
round & round the ancient elm.

II.

At dinner, tame incantation:
"God is Great, God is Good,"

but in the black city
God plays double-dutch
with girls in braids, elastic hips,
legislating feet, a sound of negatives
then flight; step a crack
break mother's back
jump one jump two
in sky so blue
On the street, small masters
of destiny until later
bowed before sleep
children abdicate power
list blessings ...

III.
God has returned to earth,
thin, long-haired, male
dripping of water, a form
a girl can believe in.
The Methodist girls have clear skin
and only rarely whisper to their boyfriends,
"this is my body which I have broken for you
this is my blood ..."
The Catholic girls learn to kneel
perfect that crossing of self
the daily gestures of faith
which at night lead to driving in parks,
peroxide hair, cigarettes and pseudonyms.
Honey, Baby, they yell to one another between lampposts
and trees, a visual guide of light and shadow.
And all hell breaks loose.

Mary, transformed, redefined, asserts herself:
It is Joseph I love, Joseph
I am on my knees before.

IV.
Mornings in Illinois I waited by the window.
Cornfields transformed into streets and
Still I refused to grow old.
Now more often it is like last night,
Misplaced and traveling
A Wyoming road
The deer moved with the car.
I moved with the deer. I stopped,
Not knowing which way to continue.
Hidden in my dome of glass,
I saw the herder and his sheep
Walking toward the hilltop
Like a pilgrim.
I called to him. I wanted to tempt him
Down from his mountain, away from
His distance of saints.

V.
The author creates distance and character—
a love-mad anorexic girl, unable
to rise from the sofa
repeats the pilgrim's one prayer.
Outside, in the world
a dog barks, the grass dies
a balding woman huddled in her shawl
shouts to passers-by they have forgotten Jesus
that unending life of tangled bones

the kiss goodmorning and goodnight,
barely enough love to starve on.
The girl arises to answer
a regular Lazarus
carefully stepping
toward the kitchen
ready to eat, grow old,
call all the children home
when the streetlights come on.

VI.
God could smother you given half a chance,
which is why
the man with the cart
still peddles umbrellas on a sunny day
and why women cover their heads
as they scurry to church.
Because I have not learned how to pray
I listen. The Joshua trees bend
toward presence unforeseen and
the twists of human language
take form. *Magnum Mysterium*,
everything I have lost
belongs to you: the winter
and its many coasts, the candles
luminous in Mexican shrines.
These are the reflections of earth
glowing through dark night:
one thousand saharas, camels
arched across landscaped cadence:
fugue, sonata, invention,
the rhythm of the blood

and the life everlasting.
Thirsty and thin, in desert
I lift my arms and give back
image: unto, unto, unto.
The galaxy circles above
wondrous beasts roam
and even under these skies
the walkings of mad men
continue in rhythm.

About the author

Gale Walden was born in Urbana, Illinois and grew up on the South Side of Chicago. She took a B.A. in music therapy and an M.F.A. in writing from the University of Arizona. She currently resides in Urbana, Illinois.